WHO SHALL I BE TODAY?

Dear Surbhi,

Be Awesome Always!

Love
Sunita

WHO SHALL I BE TODAY?

Sunita Saldhana

PARTRIDGE

Copyright © 2016 by Sunita Saldhana.

ISBN: Softcover 978-1-4828-6924-8
       eBook   978-1-4828-6925-5

All rights reserved. No part of this book may be used or reproduced by any means, graphic, electronic, or mechanical, including photocopying, recording, taping or by any information storage retrieval system without the written permission of the author except in the case of brief quotations embodied in critical articles and reviews.

Because of the dynamic nature of the Internet, any web addresses or links contained in this book may have changed since publication and may no longer be valid. The views expressed in this work are solely those of the author and do not necessarily reflect the views of the publisher, and the publisher hereby disclaims any responsibility for them.

Print information available on the last page.

To order additional copies of this book, contact
Partridge India
000 800 10062 62
orders.india@partridgepublishing.com

www.partridgepublishing.com/india

Contents

Words	1
Being a woman	2
Who shall I be today?	4
From a cygnet to a swan	5
Today I found myself again!	7
Laughing at Life	9
Today	10
Kaleidoscope	12
The mask	13
The Choice	14
Sometimes	15
Alone	16
When Silence Screams	17
Pathjhad	19
Painting over memories	20
Where is the time?	22
I see my baby walk	23
When you stop being a mom	25
Mom Grows Up	27
A daughter gets married	29
My first day in school	31
Death	32
Too young to die	34
Until	36
Dancing with your memory	37
They lie	39

Just a little glad	40
Love Beyond Understanding	42
Fear then and now	43
Fearful Freedom	44
Where emotions turn to stone ...	45
Cracks in the wall	46
The outsider	48
Pending Storms	49
What is it about love	51
Don't tell me not to love	52
He exists	53
My heart and my head	54
Dawn	56
I love you but	57

Words

Words,
My life, my love,
My constant companion,
My comfort, my joy.

Words,
Adding magic to my world,
Breathing life into feelings,
Helping me fly.

Words,
Helping me discover
Hidden facets to myself,
Defining who I am.

Words,
Defining relationships,
Giving meaning to life,
Capturing precious moments.

Words,
In poems, in songs,
In status updates, advice given,
All around.

Words,
Hurting, wounding,
Never letting me forget,
Never letting go.

Words..............

Being a woman

Being a woman
Is so much fun,
With all the nuances
That make me one.

To bring you sunshine
My smile I use,
Or appeal to your chivalry
With tears if I choose.

One flirtatious glance
And your spirits rise.
I can drive you to madness
No matter how wise.

I can make you feel strong
Though I am not weak.
And when you are low
My comfort you seek.

In anger or jealousy,
My unsheathed claws
Don't understand logic
Or rules or laws.

Don't ever even think
That you can guess my mood;
From impishly naughty
To angelic good.

With the best of minds
I can plot and scheme,
But can sacrifice it all
For your dreams.

My love can never be
Without angst or pain,
Anathema to mundane
A drama queen I reign.

I make you dance
When you want to run,
When you are intense
I add some fun.

I can talk incessantly
When you want some quiet.
And irritate you by cuddling
Close throughout the night.

My world is fun
And vibrant too,
And so much more beautiful
When I share it with you!

Who shall I be today?

Good morning mirror,
Tell me what will I see?
What mask shall I put on?
Which Sunita should I be?
Doing everything I should
Should I be obedient and good?
Or should frivolous be my choice of mood?

Am I the parent today,
Or a teacher showing the way?
Perhaps a curious innocent child,
Or a rebellious teenager running wild?
Seductive and flirtatious, a woman in love,
Or quiet and timid as a dove?
Jaded and disillusioned should I be,
Or should I be an idealistic me?

So tell me Mirror
Who shall I be?
Of the many faces of mine
Today, what will I let people see?

From a cygnet to a swan

Looking through the mirror of time
I see a much younger me.
An oh so innocent me!
At 16 she didn't know
who I would be
when I reached 43.

Naivety turned to acceptance,
Acceptance became strength.
Somewhere along the way
came the realisation
that she did not need anyone else
to fulfil her dreams.
She was enough.

And slowly over the decades,
She shed inhibitions.
She fought for what she believed.
She flowed with life,
But used the strength of the boulders
that she smashed against
to build herself.

And time and again
She was destroyed.
Only to rise again.
Till I was born.
Out of the ashes of the past,
With her ability to dream,
With her ability to love.

But with the ability
To run the race alone
If need be.
With the ability
To celebrate being myself.
To throw back my head
and laugh at the rain that threatens
and use its tears to nurture my soul.

As I look at the mirror of time
I smile, loving what I see.
A beautiful swan,
Yes, that's me!

Today I found myself again!

As I looked into the mirror,
An image stared back at me;
A tired worn out face.
I wondered who it could be.

With eyes so dull,
No life, no shine.
A mouth that was just a
Weary line.
An expression of defeat and pain,
Wary of being hurt again

I looked at her.
Who could it be?
Then with a shock I realized,
That the woman was me.

Aghast I looked!
This could not be!
This is not the person
I want to be!
When had I ceased to exist?
When had I changed to this?

For a long time
I was lost.
Lost in a maze
Of grief and pain.
But today,
I found myself again.

I was lost
In a place so dark.
But today from somewhere deep inside,
Grew a tiny spark.
A tiny spark of defiance;
A quiet surge of rebellion.
A flicker that could have died,
If I had not quickly
grasped it tight.

It rebelled against what I had become.
No I couldn't give up without a fight!
No, I would claim myself again!
Get out of this pain,
And hope again,
Start to live again.

Yes, for a long time
I was lost.
Lost in a maze
Of grief and pain.
But today,
Today, I found myself again!

Laughing at Life

And I want to laugh.
Throw my head back,
Lift my hands to the heavens,
And laugh!

A deep belly rumbling laugh!
I want to laugh,
In sheer happiness;
In resignation.

I want to laugh
Coz I've reached rock bottom.
And it's exhilarating
To feel that firm nothingness.

To know you can't go lower.
That there is nothing more to lose;
That there is nothing left
To worry about.

Now the only way is up
And forward.
Now it's exciting new dreams to dream!
New directions, new beginnings!

So many roads!
So many possibilities!
And I want to laugh
At the sheer adventure that life is!

Today

Today so much has happened.
They say we have reached Mars.
And somewhere else a filmstar
And a newspaper clash over bras.

Jammu and Kashmir still
Suffer the aftermath of the flood.
And someone posts on facebook
An urgent need for blood.

My neighbour and Bhajiwallah
Bargain over the price,
While the crows create a clamour
Over the offerings of rice.

I read, I see and listen
And pay them little heed.
And thinks instead of what
My family I will feed.

My nicest bed sheet I find
Ripped into tiny shreds
By the angelic little puppy
Looking adoringly at me from the bed.

"Mom! I'm going to be late
My bus I am going to miss!"
And my darling daughter
Leaves without a kiss.

The other news around
Seems to fade away somewhere
I know all of it
I just don't seem to care.

It is not part of my world
Of what I do or say
Just noises on the fringe
Of my busy busy day.

Kaleidoscope

And it moves again
Creating a different pattern.
Old relationships gone,
Some forever lost.

New ones just emerging,
Before they change again.
Tentative bonds,
Seeking permanence.

Beliefs once held sacred
Now crumble into nothing.
Newer thoughts form
And change and merge again.

Habits of a lifetime
Sit uncomfortably.
Different things now fill my day
What was and what is
Forming patterns;

Patterns always changing.
The kaleidoscope of life.

The mask

The day is done.
Finally alone.
Free to give in to the tears
That have been threatening all day.
There's no one to see.
No one here except me.
So the tears flow,
Allowing the sadness to show.
The hurt, the pain, the loneliness,
Things I cannot share.
Coz there's no one who really cares.

Tomorrow I'll get up,
Put on my mask again.
Yes, I'll spread sunshine and cheer
To everyone around
Smile and laugh to hide the pain.
And I'll do my crying in the rain.

The Choice

"Come!" the darkness whispers,
Comfortingly like an old friend.
"Come!" soft as a lullaby.
"Come!" enticing like the embrace of a lover.

"Come!"
The darkness surrounds, envelops, pulls
Comforting, soothing, seducing...
"Come!" just a whisper.

Suddenly
Another voice
Harsh, bright
"Live!" says life, "It's not time yet."

"Live!" she orders.
"There's work to be done."
"Come" soft, inviting.
"Live" harsh, demanding!

I look yearningly to the darkness
"Come" mockingly now,
Even as I turn
Knowing I can't resist Life
As she pulls me into the light.

Sometimes

Sometimes, just sometimes.......
I wish I could stop being responsible.
I wish that I could dance in the rain,
And chase after rainbows.

Sometimes, just sometimes.......
I wish I could read a book
Without feeling guilty
About the million things I've neglected.

Sometimes, just sometimes........
I wish that I could lay my head
On mamma's lap and cry,
Or lose myself in sleep.

Sometimes, just sometimes...
I wish I could afford the luxury
Of feeling fragile,
Of being taken care of,
Of not having to take decisions.

Sometimes just sometimes.......
I wish I had a shoulder to lean on,
A strong chest to snuggle against,
Arms to hug me.

Sometimes, just sometimes........

Alone

It steals upon you quietly,
As the evening turns to night.
And you realize you've always been alone,
There's been no one by your side.

The illusion of belonging
Shatters into pain.
And the chill of loneliness
Surrounds you once again.

You learn to use the illusion
As you live and laugh and smile.
Desperately hiding tears and feelings
That threaten to spill over all the while.

When Silence Screams

One by one they all leave
Each one on their way,
And in this lonely room
All alone I will stay.

Once the music of laughter
Rang out in happy cheer.
The patter of busy feet
And people always near.

Bonds which once were close knit
Are now threadbare and weak.
The chill comes in through the gaps
Which to fill I desperately seek.

The quietness is deafening.
It hurts my ears so!
The silence roams in madness,
As if it has nowhere else to go.

My poor thoughts try so hard
To keep me company.
But soon they start to sound
Like a boring litany.

The silence is greedy,
It doesn't spare a single thought.
It gobbles every one of them,
No matter how hard they fought.

The people, the thoughts and the words,
Each one on their way;
And alone in this screaming silence
Forever I will stay.

Pathjhad

Pathjhad....autumn.....fall....
I try out all the words as I watch the leaves fall around me.
For some strange reason the way the leaves were falling,
It seemed more like a pathjhad than anything else.
A sudden storm, the wind dashes around as I stand there,
Buffeted on all sides; physically, mentally, emotionally.

I watch the chaos of the leaves as they are tossed around.
They seem like the pieces of my life being tossed around in my head.
But then subtly,
As I look on, the pattern changes.
Now it looks like the leaves are dancing.
Twirling, soaring, dipping back before soaring away again!
And watching them my thoughts too start dancing
Twirling, soaring, dipping and soaring again!

Now, instead of getting upset by the mess in my head,
I laugh at the myriad thoughts.
The patterns being formed;
The possibilities with every twist and turn.
I stand there with my face turned up to the breeze,
Soothed by the leaves swirling around me.
Pathjhad !

Painting over memories

Today they are painting the house
after 6 years.
For 6 years
The house has stood as it was...

No......that's not true....
It had changed.
In the first year
There were random lines,
Some straight, some zigzagging,
A rainbow of colours
Randomly beautiful.

Then, a series of
          Cs
    B
A
In ascending order.

Then all the suns and moons of the universe.
And one big jolly yellow sun,
With a purple mouth,
Which Natasha said was a brinjal that the sun was eating.

They are going to paint the house.
And so today they have scrapped the walls,
Scrapped away the milestones of my life.

The 8 legged cat;
The gifts for "Mummy"
Will all be wiped out.

I stand and stare
As if to imprint the pictures
In my memory forever.

My daughters' childhood wiped out
Time flies, memories fade,
Walls get repainted.

A wave of sadness sweeps over me.
I can't hold back time.
But time is life
Would I really want to hold it back?

Where is the time?

A million things on my "to do" list.
Will they ever get done?
The squirrel scampers up the balcony railing
And asks, "Don't you want to have some fun?"
I reply, "Sure I do,
But all these things need to be fin'shed too."
Sadly, he scampers off
To find someone else to play,
While I go about
All my chores for the day.

Rumi sits on the table
Waiting to be read,
But there is a pile of ironing
Sitting right on my bed.
A dozen ideas for my blog
Play hide and seek in my head.
I tell them to wait
As I go to the market instead.

Oh no, today was the last day
To go for the movie that I wanted to see
But dinner has to be made
And even then I won't be free.
Ah finally, I can take a break
And sit down with a much needed cup of tea.
Who was I kidding?
There it comes, a screaming summons,
"Mummmyyyyyyy!"

I see my baby walk

I see my baby walk
On a road that is new.
I see her hesitate,
She doesn't know what to do.
She is in love,
And the feeling is new.
I see my baby walk
On a road that is new.

There are stars in her eyes
And her heart sings a song.
Her thoughts are of him
All the day long.
I see my baby walk
On a road that's new.
She is in love,
And the feeling is new.

Then she stumbles
And I can't do a thing,
As she feels the pain
That only love can bring.
Should I rush to comfort her?
Should I wipe away her tears?
Should I try to protect her
Like in yesteryears?

I see my baby walk
On a road that's new.
She is in love,
And the feeling is new.
I know I have to let her
Walk this road without me.
I have to let her fall and get up.
I have to let her be.

I see my baby walk
On a road that's new.
She's walking with someone
Who loves her too.
He's the one who will hold her,
Kiss away her tears,
Promise to be always there,
And allay all her fears.

I see my baby walk
On a road that's new.
I see her hesitate
She doesn't know what to do.
She is in love
And the feeling is new.
I see my baby walk
On a road that is new.

When you stop being a mom

Whoever said that labour was the worst pain in the world
Didn't know what they were talking about.

That is just the beginning;
The initiation;
The foretaste of what is to come;
The physical rending of your body.
How can that in any way compare
To the rending of your heart?
Nay sometimes it is the ripping into a thousand tiny bits.

At first the hurts are small.
Your baby tripping over;
Or banging her head somewhere,
A midnight fever that will not go down.
Anxiety and worry but not pain.

Then they grow but you don't.
You don't learn enough to let go.
You want to remain "Mummy" forever.
But your child has gone.

Your baby does not exist.
You are the only one in the world who can see her.
Through the guise of the stranger that stands before you.
You search for her in this woman
Who tells you to back off.

You can see the pain she is going through
As she works through relationships and jobs.
You want to hold her in your arms
And rock her to sleep to a soothing lullaby.

But now your arms are not enough.
Your love has become an intrusion.
And you stand there helpless
As you stare at those empty arms.

And dimly remembering
The pain you went through
When she was born
And you know that your initiation into motherhood
Was nothing compared to the pain of stopping being a mom.

Mom Grows Up

You cry.
But I can't
Wipe away your tears.

You are in pain.
But I can't
Comfort you.

I want to reach out
And touch you.
But you've built a barricade.

You pretend you're okay.
But my heart hurts
With every tear you shed.

My heart is shattered further
By your silence
Which I have to accept.

It takes all my will power
To look the other way
And not confront you.

I pretend to believe
That you are okay
It takes everything I've got.

When all I want to do
Is fold you into my heart
And keep you there, safe from hurt.

A daughter gets married

I can still remember your first kick,
The wonder of that tiny bubble of a movement within me,
The love that flooded my heart and brought tears to my eyes.

I remember how you would wake up,
With a cheerful toothless smile,
Bringing sunshine to my day.

Your first words, your first steps,
The first poem you wrote, the first book you read alone,
The delight on your face with each experience.

Yes, the smile, always the smile!
And today too I see that smile,
Wider, more brilliant than ever before.

As you stand beside the man you love,
Walking together down a new road,
A new life, a new beginning!

And once again, the love floods my heart,
Bringing tears to my eyes,
As I see how happy you are.

If there is a tinge of sadness
It's just because I am selfishly aware
That now no longer will every Christmas be shared.

No longer will this be home;
I am not the only mom in your life.
But that sadness is fleeting.

Coz I can feel the love that surrounds you,
Not only from your husband, but your whole new family.
And as you walk down the road of this new life,
All I can give you is a heart full of love and blessings!

My first day in school.

I looked across the sea of faces,
My heart a mess of a million fears;
Fifty pairs of eyes watched me,
Some curiously, and some full of tears.

All the names I had to remember;
Make myself heard above their cries.
How on earth, was I, I wondered,
Supposed to make all of them wise?

Snotty noses, bathroom trips,
Amidst ABC and 123.
Who wanted their mamma more, I wondered,
Was it the little kids or was it me?

Death

Death does not lie
Well dressed in a coffin
Surrounded by wreathes
and flowers.

Death is
The dribble of food
Down the sides of a mouth
Too weak to swallow.

Death is
The trembling of a hand
That tries to reach out
And fails.

Death is
The grimace of pain
That furrows the face
Too intense to hide.

Death is
The words crowding the mind
But which never reach the lips
Too terrified to be uttered.

Death is
The incessant beeping of the monitor
In the ICU
Counting precious moments left.

Death is
The helplessness of knowing
That your best
Wasn't enough.

Too young to die

Your eyes are closed
Do they hide the million dreams you had
But which will now remain unfulfilled?

No worry lines mar your brow.
Does it hide thoughts started
But which will now be left incomplete?

Your lips are relaxed
Do they hold the conversations begun
But which will never be completed?

As you lie there so serene
Do you regret things not experienced
Or goals unachieved?

In your last moments
Were you sad that you had to leave
this life while yet so young?

Or at the end of the day
Were you just glad
That you were free of the pain that wracked your body.

Free of the disease that
Robbed you of all that you could have had?
Of all you could have been?

While we all mourned the fact
That you were too young to die
Did you feel you had instead lived too long?

Until

Just because I love you
It doesn't mean I need you.
Can't you see
I'm getting on fine?
I've got all I need.

Until.....

That song plays on someone's radio
and catches me unawares.

Until......

I get a whiff of aftershave as someone passes by
And it seems so agonizingly familiar.

Until....

I'm watching television and a movie is screened
that I've seen years before.

Yes, I'm doing fine
just fine
don't you see?

Until.....

Something reminds me of you.

Dancing with your memory

The music plays at the party,
I get up to dance.
The song is the same.
So why do I falter?
My steps don't match,
Coz it's not you
I'm dancing with.

My feet remember your rhythm.
Without you to guide me,
The steps are strange.
My feet don't know
What to do.
They are so used to
Dancing with you.

The familiar music
The familiar steps
Are all strange and new
Coz I'm not dancing with you.

I'm alone at home
The music plays
I get up to dance
Alone.

And slip into a familiar rhythm
It is as if you are here
Dancing with me
Guiding my steps
It's so comfortable dancing alone
With my memories of you.

They lie

They say that time heals all wounds
Well they lie!

Just when you feel perhaps you'll be okay
Something else comes up,
To remind you of what can never be.

How much longer will it take
For me to feel no pain
When I remember you?

How much longer
till I forget your touch?
How much longer will it take
for me to stop wishing you were here?

The one person who knew me
better than anyone else.
How many times will I ask
Why did you have to die?
They say time heals all wounds
But they only lie.

Just a little glad

Now that you have gone
I am so very sad,
But I won't be truthful
If I don't say
I'm also a little glad.

For 30 long years
I've loved you,
More than you ever knew
And in your own way,
I know that you loved me too.

My tears are for
That love we shared,
Which lived in spite
Of everything.

That special feeling
In my life
That only you
Could bring.

But in a little corner
Of this weeping heart of mine,
A very tiny ray,
Of relief you will find.

Coz now you can never hurt me,
With those cruel words you say.
Or compare me to another
Every single day.

I'll no longer fear the beatings,
Or the lashings of your belt.
I can feel the disappearance
Of the fear that I once felt.

I no longer
Have to weigh my words,
Or feel less than I am worth.
No longer can you make me fear,
No longer can you hurt.

So now that you're gone
Though I do feel sad,
Just in a little corner of my heart
I am a little glad.

Love Beyond Understanding

"I don't understand your relationship," people tell me.
I just shake my head and say, "I know."
How can I expect people to understand what we had?
How can I tell them it's not something you'd understand
unless you've experienced it?

Passion as bright as two stars colliding
and as destructive
Love that thrilled as it frightened with its intensity.
The oneness, the belonging that was so complete one
moment
that it made us wonder who we were the next.
Soaring into the heavens in the sheer delight of love
and then the fear of doubt; wondering how this could be true.
Yes, the clashes were all fiery, whether in love or in anger.

But through it all we were together, somewhere bound
In the knowledge that the other lived and breathed
And that somewhere on the earth beat a heart that belonged
to us.
Of this we were sure.

But one heart no longer beats. And I can't burn alone.
I am a star whose fire is slowly dying day by day.
And I dream of a day when
Two stars will meet again
And colliding will create a universe of their own.

Fear then and now

Sometimes, the very fact that I am not frightened anymore
Frightens me.
I keep searching for fear like I would a friend I miss.
I've lived with her for so long
That it feels strange not to have her around.

My heart opens to love
And then hits that invisible wall
Which cautions and hold back.
Which prevents me from loving
With the innocence of the past.

And then I realise that fear is besides me once again
Only she now has a different face.

Fearful Freedom

Broken out of bars,
A taste of the blue sky,
Soaring happiness,
Someone to fly with.

Heart overflowing with love,
Singing a new song,
Surrounded by clouds,
Lost in dreams so beautiful.

Obscuring vision,
Dissipated wisps,
No one around anymore,
Illusions broken.

Lost without my bars
I return to my cage
Safe from further hurt.

Where emotions turn to stone

Deep deep down below,
Where emotions turn to stone,
Where I can never be found,
Where I can be alone.
Into the darkness of solitude,
Away from the pain,
Far from the temptation,
To love anyone ever again.

Where clamouring heart
Has no voice.
And sturdy walls
Cut out the noise.

Too tired to fight to be understood,
Too tired of being what I am not,
Too tired to fight to be me,
In a fight that cannot be fought.

Deep deep down below,
Where emotions turn to stone,
Where I can never be found,
Where I can be alone.

Cracks in the wall

One by one, they crumble,
The relationships built over years.
You thought that each brick was cemented with love and trust,
And suddenly
As if there has been a terrible earthquake,
It all comes tumbling down.

With bricks of memories scattered around
Waiting for your heart to stumble over
And start bleeding all over again.
And you realise
They don't make bandaids for bruised hearts.

You desperately try gathering the bricks,
To build again what was lost
But what emerges is an edifice
With holes in the walls
Where the bricks don't fit.

An unstable monument to the past
Which you pretend is perfect
And you know you daren't look too close
It is so much easier to paint over the cracks
with a glossy sheen of whatever shade you like

But somewhere at the edge of consciousness
you know.
And without realising it,
you wait for it to fall down again.
Knowing that when it does
your heart will be too tattered
to hold anything together again.

The outsider

You think you belong.
You call them yours.
But it's only an illusion.
Coz in reality
You are just
An outsider.

Your hopes, your dreams,
You share.
You believe they really care,
Till you hear the hidden laughter.
And you realise
You are
An outsider.

You speak the same language
Or so you seem to think
But you are left trying to fathom
What was really said.
You finally comprehend
that you're the outsider.

Words hushed when you enter
Silence heavy with emotions
What you missed was in any case
Not meant for you
Coz you do not belong
You've become
An Outsider.

Pending Storms

It's unusually still today,
And horribly hot.
Not a single leaf moves, not a single blade of grass sways.
The birds have all fallen silent.
There is a waiting, a hushed hold your breath sort of waiting.
Waiting for the storm to break, yet not knowing if it will or when it will.

In that waiting is a whisper of hope.
A hope of a respite from this suffocating stillness.
A respite from this not knowing.
A respite from the fear of what might be.
This calm before the storm.
Sometimes more terrifying than the storm itself.

Another day, another lifetime.
Standing at the window, feeling the oppressive stillness.
It has been calm for too long now.
I have been safe for almost three months.
And in this silence is the warning.
Anyday now I expect the storm to break.
I unconsciously brace myself for the blows, the lashings,
Yet I know it can be days or weeks before anything happens.
It is the knowing that it will happen,
Yet not knowing when, not knowing what will trigger it, that suffocates,
That has me holding my breath just like the leaves outside.

The thunder suddenly crashes loud outside the window,
The wind rushes around like a mad man,
The rain pelts down, relentless, battering everything with all its might.
But once spent, it disappears, leaving behind a magical world,
Full of sparkling drops on leaves and grass, containing a million rainbows.
Illusions that disappear once they dry up.
The breeze too tired of having held its breath for so long, blows gently.
The world suddenly seems so beautiful.

At home too, the storm arrives, vicious and cruel.
But having spent itself, it changes.
It is as if all the tension of the previous days has just disappeared.
As if it never happened.
The gentleness and love is poignant with regret
And though I know it is just as much an illusion as the rainbows outside,
I hold these moments close,
Knowing that I have a respite for some time at least
And I can breathe once more albeit for a little while,
Till I start dreading the build up of another storm.

What is it about love

What is it about love
That makes you want to express it?
Why can't it remain quietly,
Within the confines of your heart?

It has to creep into conversations,
Searching for openings;
To make itself known,
In subtle ways or not.

Dreams can never escape
Its merciless onslaught.
It seems to yell out to the world
Either loudly or soft.

Poems get scribbled,
Silly, stupid, juvenile.
Words have to be written,
Sensible or not.

It seems to bait embarrassment,
With its eagerness to be known;
The need to be acknowledged,
Like an addiction out of hand.

What is it about love
That makes you want to express it?
It doesn't seem to matter
Whether it is reciprocated or not?

Don't tell me not to love

Don't tell me not to laugh so loud
I have cried enough tears to last a lifetime.

Don't tell me not to believe in fairies and magic
I'm done being realistic.

Don't tell me not to dance with so much abandon
My spirit has been imprisoned for too long.

Don't tell me dreams won't come true.
I've buried enough dreams for the sake of others.

Don't tell me not to love so much
That's all that's left in my heart after getting rid of the fear.

He exists

He exists, my perfect man,
Unlike heroes in romance books
He isn't like them in character
Nor is he like them in looks.

He exists
Flesh and bone
Not just wisps of my fantasies
Dreams when I'm alone.

Though I search and search
No one else can match
The standards he sets.
"So" you ask, "what then is the catch?"

Well, you see, I've found him
The perfect man for me
But this wonderful man of mine
Still has to find me.

My heart and my head

"Not again!" grumbled my head.
"What am I to do with you?"
My heart paid no heed
As it blissfully flew.

My head reached out
And managed to hold it down
"Have you no sense?"
It scolded with a frown.

"I can't seem to help it"
Said my heart with a sigh
Whenever I see him
I just want to fly."

"But what you feel
Makes no sense at all
You're setting yourself up
For a nasty fall."

"You know this love
Can never be
It will only end
In misery."

"I didn't plan
To feel this way.
When I fell
I cannot say."

"But after so long
When I get wings,
And for no reason
I want to sing"

"Why should I stop
And put on your chains?
Why can't I
Be in love again?"

"Because it is stupid
And will only lead to pain.
Are you willing to risk
All that again?"

"He doesn't know,
And does he even care?
Are your dreams something
He is willing to share?"

And as I listen to both
Of these my dear friends
I wonder who it is
That will win in the end.

Dawn

That special time between morning and night,
It's not dark, yet not light.
Everything is a cocoon of quiet.
And no one exists but you and me.

Feel so warm and safe from fear,
The voice of responsibility not too clear.
Can we forever linger here
Just you and me?

The rules of the world don't apply.
No one asking how or why.
Condemning voices do not cry.
Just love, you and I.

Dream's wispy clouds float away
Without them you cannot stay
So starts another day
Just cold bereft me.

I love you but.......

Yes, I love you but
But that doesn't mean
That I need you to be with me all the time.

I love you but
I am happy when I am alone too.

I love you but
I enjoy being with my friends,
Even if you are not with me.

I love you but
I don't need to be always talking to you.

I love you and you make life so much better
I love being with you,
You make me smile and laugh,
You make me feel special and cared for.
But

If you are not in my life tomorrow
Though I will miss you terribly
I will still live
Every day of my life.